A Brief History of
Political Cultural Change

Eric Shierman

CreateSpace,
North Charleston, SC.

ISBN: 9781468163537

Library of Congress Control Number: 2012900881

CreateSpace, North Charleston, SC.

This book is dedicated to Bob Gillis of Portland State University and the few teaching professors like him who take up most of the burden to educate undergraduates at large universities.

Note to my readers: I would like to learn from you as well. Please send your comments to eshierman@yahoo.com.

Contents

1

an introduction to political philosophy

We live in a time of great political cultural change. To understand how this change unfolds we have to be somewhat reductionist, boiling political culture down to its most elemental level. All normative political thought can be reduced to three ideologies. Political cultural change is then the chemistry by which those three ideologies interact – how they mix, bond, and sometimes explode.

Ideologies exist as ideas within the minds of political thinkers, but to understand the unfolding of history's political cultural change, we have to understand how ideologies compete with each other in the real world by political actors. In practice, two sides compete with each other for power. How do three ideologies form two sides? At any particular point in time one ideology is dominant facing off against a coalition to the other two weaker rivals.

To understand political cultural change, we have to first make an analytic distinction between three ideologies as pure ideas which remain constant compared to the real political battles we see at unique moments in time between two sides that remain in flux.

Ideology is a universal answer to the question: "What is Just?" Regarding public policy: "What is the Good?" All three ideologies answer these questions with the same answer: "freedom." However, three different understandings of what it means to be free follow: a Conservative one, a Liberal one, and a Socialist one.

One's definition of freedom follows from one's understanding of human nature and the origin of the state found in the ideology's social contract theory. There are three different conceptions of the social contract that serve as foundations for the obligations an individual owes to the state in exchange for the rights he demands.

Conservative social contract theory was known and accepted by political thinkers and actors long before anyone ever formally wrote it down in a work of political philosophy, but the first person to do that both systematically and naturalistically was Thomas Hobbes in *Leviathan* (1651). All non-Western civilizations were unmistakably Conservative before European contact. Conservative political philosophy is itself a universal default position natural to human thought.

It remained unchallenged until the rise of
Modernity.

In Conservative social contract theory, man
is, always has been, and always will be inherently
evil. Out of the disorder of the "state of nature" (an
anarchic human society without a public system of
justice) somebody strong emerged to create order
by restraining his neighbors' threatening behavior.
To maintain order he dominated society by the
hard-power of brute force, deterring the natural
brutality of each other member of society with the
threat of greater brutality in return. This strong-man
and his tribe, clan, or allies, created a social elite in
society, putting an end to the otherwise endless
cycle of retributional violence. This dominance
developed into a monopoly of the legitimate use of
force for policing power: the "coercive power of the
state."

Shear brute force as hard-power is the
external dimension to this authority, but the elite
began increasingly to dominate society through an
internal dimension: the soft-power of cultural
supremacy. The elite began to define the sacred and
the profane so that each member of society became
knitted together as a community with shared
cultural values.

This has been the dominant understanding of
the social contract for most of human history so
Conservative societies are many and diverse.
Pantheistic societies have explained their social
contract in the context of their dependence on forces

of nature. Polytheistic societies have explained their social contract in terms of the interrelationship between the gods' competing interests and the competing interests of great men and heroes.

Monotheistic societies have explained their social contract in terms of revealed law where political authority is understood to come from the one true God. Monotheism achieved the highest development of Conservative political culture where moral standards come not from the arbitrary whims of competing gods for their parochially self interests, but rather were handed down from a loving God that defines the meaning of Truth, Beauty, and the Good, giving these rules as a gift to ancient patriarchs that have now been passed down to us so that we might live the good life as well.

Conservatives have also recognized the earthly authority of kings and an elevated class of nobility, believing they were chosen by supernatural intervention into history (providence) or as the Chinese called it "the mandate of heaven." The duty of every member of society to fill out the role God has placed upon them is emphasized over individual rights.

Liberal social contract theory was first written down by John Locke in his *Second Treatise of Government* (1690). Liberal social contract theory accepts the inherent destructiveness of man outside the order-making institutions of civilization. When people are free from the restraint of the law, so are their neighbors. In this state of nature people possess the unlimited right to use violence to defend their life, liberty, and property from any threat of attack from those neighbors. The Liberal assumes that with the aid of reason, people can come to understand that if we all give up our right to the use of violence for self-protection, to a government whose police force is devoted entirely to that end, then our life, liberty and property will become more secure, providing more time to enjoy that life, working in the pursuit of greater happiness.

Socialist social contract theory was first conceived by Jean-Jacques Rousseau in *The Social Contract* (1762). In it, humans are inherently good from the beginning. The Socialist conception of pre-civilized man is that of the "Noble Savage," where everyone was equal to all other members of society in status and material possessions. They were loving, content, and altruistic. Only under these conditions was man truly free and happy to live a natural, fulfilling life.

We lost that idyllic existence when destructive institutions emerged that corrupted humanity. First and foremost of these was the institution of private property rights. The very paradigm of property rights destroyed the naturally altruistic condition of man, placing us into a condition defined by want rather than contentment. It is thus institutions that corrupt man. If better institutions are formed, then man can become better than he is today. If perfect institutions are formed, then man can become perfect *again*. Humanity needs a new social contract that radically alters the present socio-economic order that prevails today, replacing it with a newly re-engineered one that would allow us to be altruistic, content, and loving once again.

During the 17th century, these three competing social contract theories' thought experiments amounted to cutting-edge social science, but more rigorous approaches have emerged, allowing modern anthropology to leave Hobbes, Locke, and Rousseau behind. The most authoritative summery of our modern understanding of how the state emerged is found in Francis Fukuyama's *The Origin of Political Order*. Fukuyama points out that humanity has never lived as isolated individuals. There was no point in history where we gave up our natural liberty to form the state. We were political animals from the beginning. Ideas of liberty and equality emerged later.

This positive social contract theory of contemporary social science does not negate the normative social contract theory of Enlightenment era inquiry. With the exception of various specific myths of the origins of humanity, the general Conservative understanding of human nature seems to be confirmed by the archaeological record. This helps explain why human political arrangements changed so little for so long.

Were Julius Caesar transported nearly two millennia in time to have dinner with George

Washington at Mt. Vernon he would feel right at home. Caesar would be transported to Washington's residence by wind and horse powered transportation. Their dinner would be served by slaves, and they would have lots to talk about. Social status was determined by birth. No matter how much money the small commercial interests of the cities made, it could never buy the prestige of owning a plantation. Making one's living from the soil was surpassed in status only by one other means of achievement - to prove one's honor on the battlefield.

Were we to transport George Washington a mere century into America's future he would be completely lost. By then, steam powered transportation had reduced the world's size. Slavery was illegal. Lowly born immigrants accumulated prestigious social status after building large industrial companies. Warfare had become seen as the silly preoccupation of the old world.

There is something about Modernity that made new conceptions of social contract theory possible, fundamentally changing social scientific reality and making the historical social contract irrelevant. For Enlightenment era philosophers and those who study political theory today, social contract theory acts as a thought experiment to explore the implications of normative assertions of justice. The Modern world is so fundamentally different than the ancient origins of human politics that the historical social contract provides few lessons for today's political thinkers.

All three social contract theories define the purpose of the state as the maintenance of "freedom," but they have three different understandings of what "freedom" is. For Conservatives, we are only free when we live in a stable, cohesive society. The purpose of the coercive power of the state is to maintain stability and order by mandating status hierarchies and cultural norms. Freedom is then a *positive* condition. One is free only if one *has* a tightly knit society that can sustain order. One can only be free if one is in bondage to God and duty bound to his community. The coercive power of the state exists to maintain the social bonds of the community to preserve order.

For Liberals, we are free when we are able to do whatever we want short of taking away the life, liberty, or property of any other member of society. Freedom is then a *negative* condition – the *absence* of external restraint. The coercive power of the state exists to maintain maximum individual freedom of action.

For Socialists, we are only free if we can all live up to our true potential to live fulfilling lives. Freedom is then a *positive* condition. One is only free if one *has* achieved authentic existence. The coercive power of the state exists to create new human institutions that will make this possible for everyone.

Conservatives, Liberals, and Socialists look to three different places to find the source of sovereignty for their vision of the state. Sovereignty is supreme authority within a territorial entity. What makes a government legitimately sovereign? In one sense, all governments that possess the coercive power of the state are sovereign in the classic Weberian definition when the state's authority meets a reciprocity of expectations between the government and the governed, but Max Weber's famous definition only covers the "is" of sovereignty. Ideology defines it in terms of "ought."

For Conservatives, there has been a huge diversity in specific sources of sovereignty. For religious political cultures it is of course God. Secular Conservatives agnostically find it in the anonymously timeless authority of traditional social norms. For 20th century fascists, it was the fuzzy notion of the spirit of the nation itself. They all share the same characteristic: something that transcends man as an authoritative marker of objective value.

For Liberals, sovereignty comes from the consent of the governed. It is too easy for 21st century Americans to confuse this with democracy *qua* democracy. Consent does not necessarily mean elections. It simply means the acceptance that one's life, liberty, and property are protected. If an individual does not believe that his life, liberty, and property are sufficiently protected, then rebellion against the state is *justified*. If a preponderance of the governed feel this way as to make rebellion *possible*, then the state has lost its sovereignty. The development of democracy, in Modern times, was supported by Liberals like Thomas Jefferson and James Madison as a pragmatic tool to build a feedback loop to the government so as to avoid the need for rebellion. Liberals who have supported democracy have always been conscious of the need to limit the democratic process with enough friction to prevent an illiberal "tyranny of the majority" from emerging. Liberals once called these institutional restraints on the will of the people "republicanism." It is now generally referred to as "liberal-democracy."

For Socialists, sovereignty comes from the "general will of the people," an ambiguous term that tries to capture the notion of the collective desire of all to live a fulfilling life equal in status to his neighbor. Who decides what the people actually will in general? That is the vexing question that has caused Socialists to have issues with democracy as well.

Socialists want social-democracy not liberal-democracy. Many Socialists in the past have placed little hope in democracy, because they predicted the owners of capital will posses the ability to prevent the working class from voting by imposing a false consciousness on them or perhaps prevent them from voting at all. These Socialists could call the Union of Soviet Socialistic Republics, the Democratic Republic of Germany, and the

Democratic Republic of Korea *more* democratic than the United States, with a straight face, because they would argue the USSR, DDR, and DRK gave the people what they *really* wanted. These Socialists, called Leninists, placed more hope in a party that ruled as the "dictatorship of the proletariat" acting as a "vanguard of the people" to force men to be free.

Most Socialists today look back to the 2nd International, a meeting of the world's Socialist parties, to craft a common political agenda. The 2nd International called for the founding of "social-democratic" parties to fight the owners of capital with ballots not bullets. The social-democratic parties rightly assume that the working class will always constitute a governing majority in any population, so their grand-strategy has been to transform constitutionally limited liberal-democracies into more pure direct-democracies while attempting to organize a political consciousness among the various groups of the lower classes to unite them in solidarity together.

Conservatives, Liberals, and Socialists have different understandings as to what constitutes economic justice. For the Conservative, the market should provide the material needs of the community with those needs defined by objective values that transcend the individual. For the Liberal, the market should provide the material needs of the individual as he subjectively defines his needs for himself. *Anything* that is agreed to voluntarily between economic actors, without coercion, and without taking away the life, liberty, or property of a third party, is *always* just. For the Socialist, the market itself is the problem. Economic justice would provide universal social welfare, and market forces, as we know them, cannot do this.

It then follows that Conservatives, Liberals, and Socialists have different understandings as to what constitutes illegitimate economic activity. For the Conservative, it is when market forces cause social change or moral corruption. For the Liberal, it is only when a business directly takes the life, liberty, or property from another member of society. That means that if the state can achieve the equal protection of all its members' life, liberty, and property, then there is *no such thing* as illegitimate economic activity. For the Socialist, markets are inherently illegitimate and the primary source of human misery.

Conservatives, Liberals, and Socialists have three different notions of equality. For Conservatives, socio-economic equality is a bad thing, because class distinctions and social-status hierarchies are important restraints on cultural decline. In a socially hierarchical society, a moral equality exists where everyone from the top to the bottom has an equal opportunity to achieve greatness by how well they play out their role in which providence has placed them. For Liberals, equal protection of the law is a necessary component of individual liberty, but there is nothing good or wrong with socio-economic inequality. For Socialists, socio-economic equality is a necessary component to human contentment. The equality of condition frees us from want.

Conservatives, Liberals, and Socialists even view community in different ways. For Conservatives, communities are the "little platoons" (Edmund Burke's term) that provide a natural moral compass to socialize each new member of society from generation to generation. To use another Burke line: community is a compact between those who have died with those who are alive and those who have yet to be born. Every Conservative believes he possesses objective criteria to weigh the value of one community's social arrangements as morally superior to another community's social arrangements. Liberals assume community to be whatever people do together on a voluntary basis and place no objective value judgment over one system of voluntary interaction over another. Like Conservatives, Socialists place an objective value on community, stressing that no community is a true community unless every member shares the same socio-economic status.

After studying the internal logic of Conservative, Liberal, and Socialist thought carefully, one finds that ideological conflict goes all the way down to epistemology – a theory of knowledge that tries to define what makes something "true." For the Conservative, the highest source of knowledge comes from faith and tradition.

A Conservative is critical of human reason, abstraction, and scientific empiricism. The frailty of the human mind relative to the mystery of creation and the power of its creator is emphasized. Conservative epistemology is exemplified by the intellectual environment of High Medieval Europe (11th – 14th century).

For the Liberal, the highest source of knowledge comes from science. Liberals place much faith on human rationality. The progress of human enquiry is emphasized. Liberal epistemology is exemplified by the intellectual environment of the 18th century Enlightenment.

For the Socialist, the highest source of knowledge comes from emotion. A Socialist is skeptical that anything beyond one's own feeling is nothing more than a construct of the ruling elite who dominate the culture and media (post-Modernism). The development of skills that enable one to deconstruct the knowledge that is forced upon us by the prevailing socio-economic structure is emphasized. Progress in human inquiry then is to carve out our own truth that has relevance and meaning for our own personal existence. Socialist epistemology is exemplified by the intellectual environment of 19th century Romanticism.

All political thought that appeals to justice and freedom can be boiled down to three ideologies, but is every political issue ideological?

2

political issues that are non-ideological

There are political issues that lack an ideological dimension. All three ideologies share a commitment to protecting people from murder. There were psychopathic serial killers in the population of the Soviet Union who had to be hunted down by criminal investigators. While the criminal procedures of the Soviet judicial system were no doubt different than what we find in a local US courtroom, the commitment to protect the public from the likes of a Ted Bundy remained the same.

There are anarchist strains to both Liberal and Socialist thought that reject a public system of justice, but they are merely arguing that an individual's right to self protection would be sufficient to maintain order. Because anarchists reject the state, they are beyond the scope of this book. Political philosophy is about what the coercive power of the state should be used for. Those who believe there should be no coercive power of the state have no political philosophy beyond its negation.

Some issues regarding the protection of life appear to have an ideological dimension when in fact they don't. For the most part, the debate over abortion is simply a question of whether or not a fetus possesses the legal status of any other member of society. Conservatives would insist this is a religious question, but not all religions agree on this issue. There is nothing inherent to the logic of Conservative political thought that determines *necessarily* a pro-life position on abortion; it is entirely contingent on the cultural morays a particular group of Conservatives subscribe to.

Liberals have the most diversity on the issue of abortion. Accepting the role of the state to protect life, it would seem it really is just a question of legal status to them. Many Liberals are pro-choice however, influenced by an extreme libertarian position first developed by MIT philosopher Judith Jarvis Thompson which she published in the Fall 1971 issue of Philosophy & Public Affairs in an article titled *A Defense of Abortion*. Thompson reframed the act of abortion from a killing to an eviction. Denying the duty of a person to care for another, Thompson argued that a woman has the right to evict the fetus from her body by drawing an analogy where you wake up in your bed and find yourself connected in a life support system to the world's greatest violinist. She argued you would have the right to cut the tubes on the violinist and that a pregnancy amounts to the same thing. There is nothing inherent to the logic of Liberal political thought that determines *necessarily* a position on abortion; it is entirely contingent on how a Liberal views the legal-status of the fetus or the existence of a natural right of the mother to evict her child.

Most Socialists are pro-choice as well, but for a different reason. Feminist Theory, taught in every university's women's studies department, has identified the asymmetry of responsibility between men and women in child bearing as a fundamental cause of gender inequality. If a Socialist accepts abortion as a remedy to this structural imbalance of parental responsibility, the question of whether or not the fetus possesses the legal status of a human being might become irrelevant.

Those who accept this line of reasoning value the right of the pregnant woman to her gender equality over the fetus' right to live. Naomi Wolf lucidly captures this perspective in her *Our Bodies, Our Souls* essay in the October 16, 1995 issue of The New Republic:

> It was when I was four months pregnant, sick as a dog, and in the middle of an argument, that I realized I could no longer tolerate the fetus-is-nothing paradigm of the pro-choice movement. I was being

interrogated by a conservative, and the subject of abortion rights came up. "You're four months pregnant," he said. "Are you going to tell me that's not a baby you're carrying?" The accepted pro-choice response at such a moment in the conversation is to evade: to move as swiftly as possible to a discussion of "privacy" and "difficult personal decisions" and "choice." Had I not been so nauseated and so cranky and so weighed down with the physical gravity of what was going on inside me, I might not have told what is the truth for me. "Of course it's a baby," I snapped. And went rashly on: "And if I found myself in circumstances in which I had to make the terrible decision to end this life, then that would be between myself and God." Startlingly to me, two things happened: the conservative was quiet, I had said something that actually made sense to him. And I felt the great relief that is the grace of long-delayed honesty.

There is nothing inherent to the logic of Socialist political thought that determines *necessarily* a position on abortion. A Socialist's support for abortion rights is primarily contingent on an acceptance of Feminist Theory. Socialists that do not subscribe to Feminist Theory must then decide the question of fact regarding the fetus' legal status just like everyone else.

Of the many other protection of life issues that do not have an ideological dimension, one more merits addressing since it seems at times to kindle the most passionate political flames – foreign policy. Questions of war and other foreign policies are primarily about protecting citizens from external threats with the same non-ideological earnestness that police agencies protect citizens from internal threats. When issues of foreign policy go beyond matters of national security, they are merely symbolic gestures of domestic policy such as whether or not to support UN family planning aid to developing countries that includes abortion.

There is nothing inherent to the logic of Conservative political thought that determines it to be either hawkish or dovish on national security issues. As an outspoken pacifist, William Jennings Brian was the 41st US Secretary of State, resigning in June 1915 over the hawkish tone Woodrow Wilson took after the sinking of the Lusitania. Opposition to US entry into the Second World War was the Republican position while both the fighting of that war and the rise of American military leadership of the world that followed proved to be the most popular New Deal program. The regal pageantry of the military and its ability to preserve ancient social customs no doubt appeal to a

Conservative's taste, but the actual execution of a county's external relations is entirely contingent on a political culture's assessment of threats from abroad at a particular moment in time and cannot be reduced to timeless first principles.

More than any other ideology, the Liberal's quest for limited government ought to compel him to oppose interventionism abroad as strongly as he would oppose intervention into the domestic economy, but this is all contingent on the threat perception of the moment. Fighting the Cold War amounted to a massive expansion of the federal government in the United States, yet many Liberals supported a more confrontational relationship with the Soviet Union. We have had few presidential candidates as libertarian as Barry Goldwater get the nomination of a major party. Yet in the 1968 election, he actively sought out to appear more hawkish than his social-democratic rival Linden Johnson with remarks like "Let's lob one into the men's room at the Kremlin." Ron Paul has been no less libertarian than Goldwater was, yet he has an opposite approach to American military commitments abroad. There is nothing ideological determining the differences between them. Ron Paul and Barry Goldwater have perceived and interpreted geopolitical threats differently. They also have lived in different times.

In recent memory, Socialists have held the most dovish position on American foreign policy, but this is historically contingent as well. The foreign policy views of Socialist thinkers alive today have been forged by the legacy of the anti-Vietnam War movement. Had the most social-democratic wing of the Democratic Party dominated American government to the point that we would have been allied to the Soviet Union rather than fight a Cold War against it, American progressives would likely be hawkish today, having supported an alternate American policy to overthrow right wing dictators to install social democratic regimes in their place. In this alternate scenario, the anti-war movement would have been a coalition of Conservatives and Liberals instead.

Then there were the Leninists. Bolshevik revolutionaries were opposed to imperial Russian foreign policy, but after a few decades in power there was no ideological reason not to jointly carve up Poland with Germany in a way any opportunist Czar would have approved of. Military expansion became a form of spreading Socialist revolution, making the world a safer place for the Soviet Union and in their view improving the lives of the conquered country, liberating them.

The way in which war-fighting strengthens state authority was not lost on Stalin, nor did his social-democratic cousins in the West fail to see the political power of patriotism. In the United States, the social-democratic administrations of Woodrow Wilson and Franklin Roosevelt knew how to harness the organizing power of a war effort toward domestic progressive ends when they successfully fought the two world wars.

Ideology only provides domestic policy prescriptions while foreign policy merely protects domestic policy. Having said that, an expansive foreign policy is congruent with an expansive domestic policy so Conservatives and Socialists face less disadvantages from more interventions in foreign affairs. Liberals need a very high threat perception to justify a hawkish foreign policy since the warfare state tends to reinforce the welfare state.

On questions of liberty and property, there are three different systems of thought asserting notions of justice, but the protection of life is non-ideological. From abortion to foreign policy, there are many complex questions of fact that keep these issues hotly debated, but there is little normative ground to support a policy position one way or another.

3

how three ideologies form two political sides

In the world of ideas, political ideology exists in three separate forms that seek to move society in three equally opposite directions. The actual instantiation of political ideology in the real world plays out as a struggle between two sides of a political culture: a left and a right, but who is left-wing and who is right-wing changes over time.

Why can't we have a three-sided political culture? Think of a three-way tug-of-war game with a circular rope. Once the game begins, the slack of the rope tightens, turning the circle into an equilateral triangle where each corner is an ideological team pulling in its own unique direction. When one ideology becomes dominant enough to proceed in its own direction, it must then drag the other two ideologies along with it. The rope between those two weaker ideologies slackens, bringing their points closer together – eventually creating one line instead of three. Then the tug-of-war game changes from a three-way to a two-way struggle. In the ideological tug-of-war of Modern political cultures, there will rarely be three discernable ideologies competing in a trio-debate. Ideology exists, in the real world, as a duel between two sides: the dominant ideology versus a coalition of the other weaker two.

Of the few in history who come close to advocating an ideology close to its perfect form, the best place to find them is among political thinkers who act as observers and are disconnected from the political process. The worst place to find a distinct ideologue is among political actors who are forced to make pragmatic compromises once they choose to carry on the burden of the coercive power of the state.

The thinkers of the dominant ideology will be at the peak of their ideological purity. Most of the compromising occurs among the other two ideologies that are forced into a coalition.

The compromises between the two weaker ideologies are often so complete that, at any particular moment in history, it will seem as though they are, and always have been, one. When the Conservative ideology is dominant, Liberals and Socialists seem united as secular-humanist republicans against the monarchs, aristocrats, and official state clergy. For example: when the French Revolution broke out, few contemporaries could distinguish its ideological difference from the American Revolution.

When the Liberal ideology is dominant, Conservatives and Socialists seem united as defenders of human dignity against the heartless forces of an unfettered market. For example: the participation of Conservative William Jennings Brian within the Progressive movement seemed natural at the time. Union lawyer Clarence Darrow worked hard to deliver organized labor's votes to Brian's many campaigns for President.

We are more familiar with the falling out of that relationship when Brian prosecuted John Scopes for teaching evolution and Darrow represented Scopes. Between the time when Brian lost his last election in 1908 to Taft and the 1925 Scopes trial, America had undergone a significant realignment in its political culture. Before 1917 Liberalism was dominant and evangelical Christians were more concerned with the Social Darwinism of free markets.

When Socialist ideology is dominant, Liberals and Conservatives seem united as defenders of proven social arrangements against radical social-engineering. For example, in the 20th century's ideological dynamic when social democracy became the dominant ideology in the West and Leninist Socialism held dominant elsewhere, "conservatives" were Liberals and Conservatives forced into a coalition. Much of our political debate today remains influenced by the habits of this previous era, but that era's coalitions are beginning to shift.

The difference between the political cultural dynamic Brian and Darrow faced in 1908 and 1925 is illuminating. By 1925 Socialism was on the rise and the Progressive movement no longer needed its Conservative allies. Brian won the Scopes trial but fundamentalist Christianity lost in the court of elite public opinion, evicting the Conservative Protestant church from power. These churches remained withdrawn from American politics for decades until a young evangelist named Billy Graham successfully argued that the atheistic threat of global Communism was a force of evil that Protestants must resist. This transformed Conservative Christian attitudes towards economic policy from a rejection of free markets at the beginning of the 20th century to becoming a seemingly wholly owned subsidiary of the Republican Party by century's end.

There is no permanent, natural alliance among the three ideologies. When one is dominant the other two naturally merge together to maintain parity.

4

why there are two political sides regardless of party system

When a political culture is described as having two sides it would be wrong to assume this means two political parties like the two-party system so familiar to the English speaking world. A duopoly of two viable political parties is what inevitably emerges from a single-member-district electoral structure. When only one person can represent a single geographical area, more ideologically pure third parties merely take votes away from their more centrist brethren which can only help elect an opponent from the opposite side of the political spectrum.

Nationally these two centrist parties will have a diversity of ideological orientation within their own party when politicians from different regions are contrasted. For example, in the United

States during the 1970s, New England Republicans were more Liberal on civil rights issues than not only their own party members from other regions but southern Democrats as well. In a two-party system, one party will lean closer to the dominant ideology of the time while the other party will be a coalition of the weaker two.

In the competition for control over the coercive power of the state, there will always be two political sides in every political culture regardless of whether the electoral structure is a single, two, or multi-party system. This is counter intuitive to most people so let's take a closer look at one-party and multi-party systems.

There are three ways to analytically break down one-party systems, but in every permutation a single ruling party provides the only path for a political actor to enter politics, so the governing party itself becomes a *de facto* state institution. One-party states fall in between two extremes where either a single man dominates a party to the point where there is no final-authority beyond his charismatic personality or a strong party rules with final-authority over its current leader. Most one-party states are usually closer to strong-party rule. Truly single-man, charismatically-ruled, one-party states like the governments of Stalin, Hitler, and Saddam are rare. When they do occur, these governments essentially eliminate ideology beyond what ever internal ideological plurality there is in the party leader's head.

The reason this distinction remains important is that most Americans mistakenly group all one-party states into a vague "dictatorship" category and assume that there is no ideological competition within them. This has blinded both the American public and many American political analysts to the sweeping ideological change that took place in the Soviet Union and that is transforming China today. When a one-party state has a strong party that appoints and oversees its leaders, a two faction dichotomy will emerge within the party: the hardliners verses the reformers. The hardliners will be the ideology that has most recently been dominant. The reformers will be a coalition between the two other ideologies that have been marginalized.

A second characteristic of a one-party state is whether or not the law excludes other political parties or if the dominant party simply holds a natural monopoly. Not all one-party states actually exclude other political parties. Many one-party states have no formal laws that bar electoral competition, but historical circumstances allow a natural monopoly to emerge (such as the US Democratic Party of the South until 1972, the Institutional Revolutionary Party in Mexico until 2000, and the Liberal Democratic Party in Japan until 2009). In either case, because there is only one path to enter government, the governing party itself becomes a *de facto* state institution, and all power seeking individuals, regardless of their true ideological identity do and say whatever is necessary at the time to gain party membership, but can later change its policy once they emerge into the leadership, ensuring that the party is subject to normal forces of political cultural change.

A third way to classify one-party systems is whether or not the ruling party is separate from government. If there is no separation of party and government, the role of the party, as a state institution, is more direct. The party functions like a military organization with a formal rank structure and a clear status distinction between a party member (cadre) from the rest of society like the military mindset of soldier vs. civilian. Holders of government offices can be fired at the party leadership's whim and each party leader has a clear chain of command all the way to the general secretary of the party who is the *de facto* head of both the state and government. In this case the actual government simply serves as a mouthpiece for the party. The political bureaucracy (politburo) of the party organization ends up becoming the real government.

In this case where there is no separation between party and government, ideological change will be slower due to the strong institutional resistance to change that is natural to all complex bureaucratic organizations. Single-party rule that separates party and government by appointing politicians to office, but then giving them autonomous governing authority for the duration of their term are able to more nimbly govern their people but are also susceptible to more swift ideological change.

If there is any electoral process where we would expect to find more than two sides it would be multi-party systems, but they have only two sides as well. A broad array of small, extremist parties that focus on a handful of policies which their supporters consider priority issues is the hallmark of a multi-party system. Such a system only emerges as the result of proportional representation voting.

Unlike single-member district electoral structures, in proportional representation votes are cast for a party on a national level not for a person at the district level. The percentage of votes that a party gets will determine the percentage of seats that it gets in the legislature. The party then decides who will fill those seats. The two most prominent examples of this are Italy and Israel.

After the election, something interesting happens when it is time to govern. A coalition must be formed to pass legislation and, in the case where the executive branch is parliamentary, a coalition is required to form a government. This need to form coalitions turns a multi-party state into two competing coalitions which will end up being a group of those various parties who lean closer to the dominant ideology of the time vs. a group of those various parties who lean closer to the two weaker ideologies.

The ideological orientation of a country transcends its electoral structure. One-party, two-party, and multi-party systems are all two-sided ideological conflicts subject to the same forces of political cultural change.

5

where we have been and where we are going

Historically, there have been only four shifts in ideological dominance. Conservative political thought has been dominant for most of human history. Its rise follows the beginning of the state with the Neolithic Revolution. Because Conservative thought was universal, political conflict did not have the ideological element of Modern politics. Faction fought faction; even revolutions occurred, but each faction or succeeding revolutionary shared an unmistakably Conservative character with his opponent. That is the ironic meaning behind the phrase: "The king is dead! Long live the king!"

Liberalism emerged with Capitalism. It is unclear whether at 1665, Newton's integral (which made the modeling of non-linear relationships possible) or at, 1494 Pacioli's double entry-accounting (which made the corporation possible) are the deciding structural differences between Early Modern Europe and other earlier near misses, that allowed Modernity to survive against the onslaught of mytho-poetic reaction. It is clear that Liberalism emerged dominant when those two trends converged in a big way with the Industrial Revolution.

The point of no return, for Liberalism's dominance, occurred in 1848, when the British House of Commons first reformed the "Corn Laws," leading to an eventual policy of unilateral free-trade with the rest of the world. The price of agricultural produce and land fell. The power of the Conservative, landed aristocracy fell with it. The lower cost of living that followed freed up the purchasing power of consumers that increased demand for the latest, novel manufactured goods. On its face, this looks like nothing more than a transfer of wealth from one interest to another, but it entailed far more: a transfer of power from one set of ideas to another.

The Liberalism of the 19th century came to a loud end with the guns of August 1914. The First World War undermined Liberalism in three ways. First, the need for centralized authority to wage the war strengthened the power of the public sector. Second, the price of the war debt left a weak global financial architecture that finally crumbled in 1929. And third, Imperial Russia's defeat made the Bolshevik Revolution possible.

The Soviet Union that emerged was a "city on a hill" for Socialism, making it the dominant global ideology for the next 70 years. To be sure, the social-democratic parties in the West followed a different path, trying to organize peaceful political change within the constitutional parameters of their respective countries. We will all be Socialists one day, they thought, we just don't have to be mean about it like the Soviets. Across the free-world, the social-democrats reached the peak of their power in the 1970s. At the same time however, the Soviet economy was in imminent, catastrophic collapse, which would take the social-democrats down with it.

Moments of Dominance
Conservative: 10,000 BCE - 1846
Liberal: 1846 – 1914
Socialist: 1917 – 1991
Liberal: 1991 – Present

After 1991, the intellectual vacuum that the Soviet Union left behind is being filled by a new Liberal dominance – a Neo-Liberalism that is now riding a second great wave of scientific and commercial innovation. Just as science and corporate organization converged to start an Industrial Revolution that propelled Liberalism into dominance in the 19th century, today scientific progress in information technology and complex corporate finance are allowing a new, stronger global Capitalism to emerge. The Digital Age is the new Gilded Age. Just as the removal of the Corn Laws, in Britain, eliminated the political strength of the Conservative opposition within the confines of the nation-state, so too are the elimination of barriers to trade, investment, and immigration across sovereign borders eliminating the political strength of the social-democratic parties on a global level. The power of global financial markets has shifted the debate away from a social-democratic vision to increase regulatory scrutiny of industry and expand entitlement programs to a defense of what policy gains the social-democrats made back in the 1970s. As Chris Hedges likes to say, Richard Nixon was the last progressive American President.

The social-democratic parties of the West are finding it harder and harder to defend the 20th century welfare state against a more Liberal political culture that reflects a more Liberal social elite. In *The Clash of Civilizations*, Samuel P. Huntington called it the "Davos culture" after the World Economic Forum held every year in Davos, Switzerland. Davos is an informal meeting of the world's multinational corporations' CEOs, financiers, public intellectuals, and representatives of the world's governments who get together and talk about how to reduce the friction in the global economy that political borders cause.

In a 1989 paper *What Washington Means by Policy Reform* John Williamson coined the perfect term to describe the Liberal ethos of the end of the cold war: the Washington Consensus. Williamson used the term to summarize the commonly shared themes among policy advice by Washington-based think tanks and the global institutions that earnestly seek their advice such as the International Monetary Fund, World Bank, and U.S. Treasury Department: free-trade, removal of capital controls, and the privatization of state-owned enterprises.

We can measure the rise of this Neo-Liberal dominance by tracking the rise of a demographic group that is growing in size, dominance, and even prestige: the professional multinational corporate officer. If one looks at the resumes of the CEOs of the world today, one would mostly find degrees in engineering, arts, and sciences. Only among the youngest would one find a few business degrees. That is because business departments were either nonexistent or unpopular among students when this generation was of undergraduate age. Decades ago, in a time of Socialist ideological dominance on American campuses, who would study something so crass as business? Now the most popular department for undergraduates to major in is business.

At the graduate level, the MBA of every university's school of business administration is becoming as high-status a professional credential as has, in the past, been that of the JD of the school of law and the MD of the school of medicine. As the MBA becomes a gateway into a distinct profession of multinational corporate management and global finance with its own internal professional logic, and as the MBA becomes a clearer ticket to incomes and responsibilities that dwarf that of the doctor and the lawyer, it is eclipsing them in social prestige as well.

As Liberals become more organized and self aware, Socialists are becoming more divided. To be a social-democrat after 1991 is to be a defender of the welfare state against the leadership of one's *own* party's plans to reform it. This has been tearing the old left apart. To identify the origin of this trend, just watch out for the word "new." Bill Clinton called himself a "New Democrat." In the UK, Tony Blair called his agenda "New Labor." In Germany, Gerhard Schröder called his leadership of the SPD the *"Neue Mitte,"*(the new middle) and in France they did not call themselves new, but Lionel Jospin's Socialist Party legislated for France in the same new way. What is this new way? Although they would never say this out loud, it is the Washington Consensus.

This new, more Liberal, orientation of the world's social-democratic parties is an attempt to appeal to that new voting block the Davos Man. The more conscious the Davos Men become of their Liberal ideology, the more Libertarian social-democratic politicians have to become to get their vote, and more importantly their campaign contributions.

The social-democratic parties cannot please both the Davos Men and their progressive base simultaneously. Al Gore was the first to suffer the consequences. In 2000, Gore never would have had a close race to dispute had Ralph Nader not taken the most devout of his base from him. Ralph Nader called the New Democrats the "Wall Street Democrats." In 2004, despite the highly passionate opposition of his party against the war in Iraq to serve as a uniting principle, John Kerry could never energize his base the way Howard Dean could have, but Howard Dean could not have hoped to get George Soros to finance a 527 group like ACT.

The US Democratic Party's social-democratic cousins in Europe have paid a similar price. France has two national elections for president. The second election is a run-off between the top two candidates of the first election. In 2002, many French Socialists took the opportunity to send a message to Jospin by giving a protest vote to the French Communist Party in the first election. Unfortunately for Jospin, too many did so, and he did not even get enough votes to qualify for the run-off election. The French Presidential Election was between the Gaullist Jacques Chirac and the even more Conservative National Front candidate Jean-Marie Le Pen. The same process played out internally in the UK and Germany where Tony Blair and Gerhard Schröder have been forced out, leaving their parties in divided shambles.

The only example that seems to buck this trend is the election of Barack Obama in 2008 – or is it? The combination of two unpopular wars and an imminent recession provided the progressive base of the Democratic Party the opportunity to pick their dream candidate knowing that there would be a very slim chance a Republican could win in that environment. What these social-democrats needed was tangible proof that their next candidate had uncompromising authenticity to demonstrate his ideological purity.

Opposition of the war in Iraq, in 2003 when it was popular, became the litmus test to provide the evidence. This excluded Obama's most prominent rivals because they had all supported the war. Hillary Clinton was plagued by a viral YouTube clip of her arguing with Code Pink activists about her need to protect New Yorkers. The fact that there wasn't a domestic policy issue to decide the Democratic Party's presidential primary demonstrates the depth to which the social-democratic agenda has fallen.

What is so remarkable about American social-democracy's limited success in 2008 is how short it lasted. Mere months after Obama's reelection something unprecedented happened: middle class people marched and rallied in public demonstrations in opposition to what proved to be a remarkably modest Obama administration legislative agenda. The emergence of the Tea Party came so suddenly and so unexpectedly that few reporters and even fewer politicians of either party understood how uniquely Liberal a phenomenon it was. It was truly a historical milestone so see mass demonstrations demanding austerity during a recession.

What made the Tea Party even stranger was its non-elite origin. The Republican Party has been able to turn people out to rallies just like the Democrats have, but only for the Conservative issues of the religious right or national security enthusiasts rallying for war. The Republicans have never been able to put people on the street marching in such large numbers to reduce government spending.

The spontaneous eruption of the Tea Party speaks volumes about the rise of Neo-Liberalism in the post Cold War world. The Obama administration ended up punting out of "the public option" of its health care reform effort on the first down of the first quarter as the Tea Party grew its momentum when he was at the height of his popularity.

As a mass movement on the populist level however, the Tea Party seems to have petered out. Emerging as a Libertarian movement that rejected the big government Conservativism of George W. Bush, the Tea Party grew out of the social media networks of the 2008 Ron Paul campaign. Being the only game in town, it soon attracted more Conservative minded Republicans to become a mass movement that demanded non-compromising ideological purity. Now those internal contradictions have become more salient. As a broad coalition, the Tea Party lost its momentum when it became a Conservative movement losing its earlier Neo-Liberal identity. This was to be expected, because ultimately the dominance of Liberal ideology will be elite driven.

It is the Davos Men on whom Liberal dominance will be maintained. The dominant ideology emanates from high culture. When Liberalism was dominant before the First World War, Social Darwinism was considered a good thing within the ivy covered halls of academia. When Socialism became dominant, the same term became a political insult. In the rise of Neo-liberalism, universities, the media, and polite upper-class culture will once again accept and promote classical Liberal values – a social and cultural environment that James Piermont Morgan would recognize.

Even in the late 20th Century, we were not that far away from such a world. The Davos Men in America remained quite Liberal; their influence was simply divided amongst the two political parties. Davos Men who cared more about economic liberties were Republicans; those that cared more about civil liberties were Democrats. A world in which they can care about both at the same time is not impossible to imagine.

Were the Davos Men to have one political party that fully reflected both their civil libertarian and free-market values; it would be a party of elites that would find its majorities in what we identify as "blue states" today. The preponderance of

America's elite, often called "limousine liberals," have supported the Democratic Party. Most of this support however has gone toward culture war, anti-war, and environmental causes – save the whales not save the workers.

The political success of organized labor in the United States has been in its coalition with the Liberal side of the culture wars, often against its own rank and file's values. It will not be difficult for the Davos Men to end this relationship with the labor movement nor will it be difficult for the labor movement to enter into a new coalition with culturally Conservative groups that their membership already disproportionately supports.

The Occupy Wall Street movement has offered frustrated Socialists their own mass movement. Just as the Tea Party was initially a reaction to big government Conservatism, the Occupy movement was really a reaction to the Davos Men's influence on the Obama administration. They are after all the 1%. This has pushed Obama into a populist direction that threatens to sever his ties to the Davos Man establishment. University educated professionals who make up the highest income earners are a critical component of the Democratic Party's demographics. How will Obama compensate for the loss of such a critically reliable voting bloc? Democrats will have to build on the 2006 elections when they began pioneering an economically populist message tied to culturally conservative candidates. Bob Casey's defeat of Rick Santorum provides the model. This would then push the Davos Men into the laps of the Republican Party.

The consolidation of the Davos Men into one party will result in a breakup of the familiar Conservative / Liberal coalition. Conservative political thought was actually quite Liberal towards the end of the 20th century. When traditional values were threatened by social engineers, to defend traditional values, all a Conservative had to do was ask that the state no longer try to stamp them out. Once given a more empowering coalition with organized labor, evangelical Christians will start to demand social engineering in their favor.

Globalization will be the fault line that alienates former free-market supporting Conservatives from the fold. The people living in what we currently identify as "red states" will reject globalization for a diversity of reasons: from the evangelical Christian's paranoia over a "one-world government" to the nationalist's desire to protect sovereignty and culture.

Beyond these non-economic concerns, protectionist sentiment already runs high in red states. It will be easy for the Davos Men and their blue states to be seen as the disproportionate beneficiaries of the free movement of products, capital, and labor across borders at the expense of the average American in the red state heartland.

Liberal thought within in the 20th century's Conservative / Liberal coalition remained limited to economics which their Conservative allies adopted and made their own. Liberals in the United States were of course called "conservatives." Only the most pure in ideology called themselves Libertarian. In the 20th century, the logic of Libertarianism's extreme tolerance was largely ignored but will now become reemphasized. Libertarians will become louder advocates for the legalization of drugs, the separation of church and state, gay rights, physician-assisted suicide, and the lowering of restrictions on obscenity in the media.

In the Republican Party of the past 30 years, those who call themselves "social conservatives" call the Davos Men in their party "country club Republicans." Davos men like Tom Ridge, Colin Powell, George Pataki, Chris Christie, Mitch Daniels, and Rudolph Giuliani tend to be pro-choice on abortion, have no qualms with gay marriage, find sodomy laws downright backward, and when one mentions the UN do not think of black helicopters flying out of Yellow Stone stealing national treasures. This rift has primarily correlated to a socio-economic divide within the Republican Party. Davos Republicans are a blue-blooded group that believe in free markets, but are also multicultural, tolerating everything but "social conservatives" on whom they look down on with thinly veiled derision.

The consequence of a new Liberal establishment will be the emergence of what will become an opposition Conservative / Socialist coalition. At this moment, the Liberals are divided among the two 20th century political parties, but this will change once one of them, or a new party, makes a successful leap for both Conservative and Socialist factions who feel more and more alienated by their own elite dominated party. Then these Davos Men will all gravitate to one secular, free-market party.

For the Conservative, the moral decline of society will more and more become blamed on global Capitalism and the individualism and selfishness that freer markets will be seen as encouraging. They will be more and more alienated by the Republican Party that will continue to focus more on the concerns of the Davos Man while continuing to take their votes for granted with little in return.

For Socialists, the way in which market forces corrupt humanity will more and more be seen in terms of traditional morality. They will wonder if the rise of materialism is due to a break-down of the family. Those old family-owned small farms or family-owned local mom-and-pop merchants may not have been Noble Savages, but they were members of a tangible community. Religion may remain a falsehood to the most pure Progressives, but it will become accepted as a noble lie that unites humanity in a brotherhood where all are equal before God. Socialists will be more and more alienated by the New Democrats that will continue to focus more on the concerns of the Davos Man while continuing to take their social democratic votes for granted with little in return.

The new alignment will be a conflict between a "libertarian" party and a "communitarian" party. This libertarian party will be the party of global community and shareholder value, whose platform will be broadly Liberal in ideology, free-market, tolerant, cosmopolitan, multicultural, secular, and dominant. So the same people who support the ACLU will support tax-cuts, limited government, and deregulation. This will either be the Republican Party or the actual Libertarian Party of today will rise to replace it if the loss of Conservatives terminally sends the GOP to RIP with the Federalists and the Whigs.

The communitarian party will be the party of local community, stakeholder value, and family values, whose platform will be broadly both Conservative and Socialist in ideology, demanding trade protectionism, reregulation, economic interventionism, patriotism, and evangelically religious symbolism in the public square. So the same people who worry about the moral decay of society will also worry about the gap between the rich and the poor. This will most likely be the Democratic Party returning to its late 19th century roots. When given this choice, which party will you vote for?

6

Conclusion

Once we understand political ideology in its elemental forms and how these systems of thought mix and match over time, we can understand political cultural change. Political ideologies are very slow to change, and have only done so a handful of times since the intellectual rise of "isms" in the Industrial Revolution. As these realignments occur, loyalty and labels become confusing as they are becoming now.

Ideological conflict is confusing because there are three equally opposed systems of normative political thought: Conservative, Liberal, and Socialist whose internal logic determines three equally opposed definitions of freedom, purpose of the state, source of state sovereignty, economic justice, illegitimate economic activity, equality, community, and even epistemology. In real political cultures, one ideology is dominant at any particular time in history, forcing the other two into a coalition to maintain parity. Since 1991, Liberalism has been reemerging at the dominant ideology and will force Conservatives and Socialists to unite once again into a coalition just as they did in the days of William Jennings Brian.

Just because Liberalism will be the dominant ideology does not mean it will actually dominate. If you are not a Liberal take heart. When Socialism was dominant in the 20th century, the coalition of Conservatives and Liberals often proved to be stronger. Liberal Davos Men no doubt command great resources and the control of cultural institutions like the media and higher education, but they are after all a minority of the population. A coalition of evangelical churches and labor unions could very well prove to be much stronger. We could very well be standing upon the threshold of a new progressive movement that will be even more successful than its forefathers.

It is also important to keep in mind that the two parties will still be centrist. A more libertarian Republican Party will not be as pure as the current Libertarian Party. It will simply match the policies of Paul Ryan and Ron Wyden on more than just Medicare. Imagine a party that holds Ryan's commitment to limited government and Wyden's commitment to civil liberties. That is basically a moderately centrist libertarianism that will not please everybody at the CATO Institute.

Similarly, a communitarian Democratic Party will not necessarily please everyone at the Family Research Council and the AFL-CIO. We can thank that Liberal James Madison for giving us a constitution that gives us either gridlock or compromise. This more populist Democratic Party will be centrist as well, matching the cultural-issue policies of Rick Santorum with the economic policies of Sherrod Brown (who actually already represents red state Ohio today).

Getting the more committed activists to march together will be more awkward. Keep your eyes peeled for old Marxist intellectuals and young evangelical Christians working together. An anti-globalization march would be a good place to start.

Europe is where the big changes will be seen. The old continent of Europe is both less democratic than the United States as well as having less checks and balances in their constitutional structures to allow for parties in power to make more sweeping changes.

They are less democratic in the sense that European politicians are not subject to anti-incumbent populist rage the way American politicians are. European voters have consistently higher turnout rates than their American counterparts but are more deferential to technocratic elites to manage public affairs. There is nothing in Europe like Fox News or talk radio driving a national debate among carpenters and truck drivers over matters of public policy. Europeans don't make mass donations to think tanks or even give much to politicians. This will allow an elite driven change toward more Liberal policies to face little more than demonstrations in the streets that will fail to translate into an organized opposition.

European constitutions are nearly universally parliamentary, meaning that there is no separation of powers between the legislative and executive branches. Few European countries have Marbury v. Madison style judicial review. When Liberal political parties are voted into office, they are able to make sweeping changes with even narrow simple majorities. The degree to which the Thatcher government of the UK reformed social democratic Britain could never be matched by her American counterpart. Reagan talked a good game, but accomplished remarkably little in comparison.

Swedish Socialism lives only in myth following the sweeping reforms of the Carl Bildt government that privatized their post office, public pensions, and its health system. Few Americans realize Sweden has become a more free economy than our own in many respects. Since Bildt's single term in government from 1991 to 1994, Sweden now has school choice and by American standards an almost unregulated economy.

Thatcher and Bildt were responding to economic crisis the likes of which the United States has yet to face. Now Europe faces an even greater challenge; social democracy may be facing its 1989 moment. The sovereign debt crisis could very well be to social democracy what 1989 was to the Soviet centrally planned economy. Sweeping Neo-Liberal reforms seem inevitable and will likely take outside observers by surprise. Every time political cultures change all involved get taken by surprise.

Suggested Reading in Chronological order

Conservative:
Thomas Hobbes *Leviathan*
John C. Calhoun *Selected Writings and Speeches*
William Jennings Brian *Cross of Gold Speech*
CS Lewis *The Abolition of Man*
Richard Weaver *Ideas Have Consequences*
Russell Kirk *The Conservative Mind*
Robert Nisbet *The Quest for Community*
Robert Bork *Slouching towards Gomorra*
David McCullough *John Adams*
Rick Santorum *It Takes a Family*

Liberal:
John Locke *Second Treatise on Government*
Thomas Jefferson *The Declaration of Independence*
Fredrick Bastiat *The Law*
John Stewart Mill *On Liberty*
Ludwig von Mises *Liberalism*
Ayn Rand *Atlas Shrugged*
Friedrich Hayek *The Constitution of Liberty*
Robert Nozick *Anarchy, State, and Utopia*
David Boaz *Libertarianism: A Primer*
Tom Palmer et al. *The Morality of Capitalism*

Socialist:
Jean-Jacques Rousseau *The Social Contract*
Marx and Engels *The Communist Manifesto*
Erich Fromm *Escape from Freedom*
Max Horkheimer *The Eclipse of Reason*
The Port Huron Statement
Theodor Adorno *Negative Dialectics*
Robert Reich *Locked in the Cabinet*
Antonio Negri and Michael Hardt *Empire*
Chris Hedges *The Death of the Liberal Class*
Katherine Vanden Heuvel *The Change I Believe In*